Gangs

JILLIAN POWELL

FRANKLIN WATTS
LONDON • SYDNEY

First published in 2009
by Franklin Watts

Copyright © Franklin Watts 2009

Franklin Watts
338 Euston Road
London NW1 3BH

Franklin Watts Australia
Level 17/207 Kent Street
Sydney, NSW 2000

Series editor: Sarah Peutrill
Editor: Sarah Ridley
Art director: Jonathan Hair
Design: www.rawshock.co.uk
Picture research: Diana Morris

Dewey number: 302.3'4

ISBN 978 0 7496 8832 5

Printed in China

Franklin Watts is a division of Hachette Children's
Books, an Hachette UK company.
www.hachette.co.uk

Picture credits: Mikhail Basov/Shutterstock:17. Barry Batchelor/PA Photos: 11. Blend Images/Photoshot: 10. Joanne O'Brien/Photofusion: 28. Graham Burns/Photofusion: 13. Elena Elisseeva/Shutterstock: 23. Fay De Gannes/PYMCA/Rex Features: 21. Kerry Garvey/Shutterstock: 18. John Giles/PA Photos: 24. Mark de Gruchy/Alamy: 19. Image Source/Rex Features: 15. Ed Kashi/Corbis: 22b. Douglas Kirkland/Corbis: 25. Olga Mirensha/Shutterstock: 29. Keith Morris/Photofusion: 5. Dino O/Shutterstock: 22t. Paramount/Kobal Collection: 12. Rex Features: 14, 20. Jamie Robinson /PYMCA: front cover, 1, 8. Paula Solloway/Photofusion: 27. UPPA/Photoshot: 9. Tracey Whiteside/Shutterstock: 4, 16. Janine Wiedel/Photofusion: 6. Every attempt has been made to clear copyright. Should there be any inadvertent omission please apply to the publisher for rectification.

CONTENTS

Look out for these features

IN FOCUS

A more detailed information panel.

ROLE PLAY

An opportunity to get together with some friends and each take a point of view and follow it through.

YOUR CALL

An invitation to explore your own feelings.

?

Dilemma
Focus on someone's difficult decision and think how you might advise them.

FOR! **AGAINST!**

Look at both sides of the argument and see which you agree with.

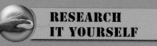

RESEARCH IT YOURSELF

Some topics that you could research yourself, either in the library or on the Internet.

About gangs

 A gang is often just a group of friends who meet up to do things together. Gangs may live in the same area, go to the same school or share the same interests. However, some gangs get mixed up in crime or make trouble in an area.

Good gangs

Young people like to spend time with their friends. They enjoy each other's company and are interested in the same things. They have fun and they feel safe together. They know their mates will look out for them.

Bad gangs

There are some gangs that like to frighten, bully or hurt others because it makes them feel powerful. They become rivals with other gangs and get into fights with them. They can also get involved with crimes, like theft and drug dealing, and be nasty or violent to anyone who gets in their way.

Most gangs of young people are not problem gangs. Many people just get together to have fun with their friends. But the fear of problem gangs can sometimes make life difficult for any group of young people in a community.

 **Super gangs**

Some street gangs (Latinos, Crips and Bloods) that began in Los Angeles, USA, have become 'super gangs' with thousands of members throughout the USA, as well as in Canada, South Africa and Europe.

During our lives, we can belong to different gangs at school, college and work.

Belonging to a gang means you always have friends to spend time with.

 If a gang wanted you to join them but you knew they bullied others, what would you do? Do you think it would be safer to join the gang or walk away?

ARGUMENTS FOR AND AGAINST GANGS

FOR!

- Being in a gang is a normal part of growing up.
- Gangs can help young people feel safe.
- People in gangs look out for each other.
- Gangs can be like families.
- Gangs stop children feeling lonely.

AGAINST!

Some gangs can:
- bully others, or make people feel uncomfortable or unsafe
- get involved with crime
- create no-go areas in a community
- fight with rivals, causing injury or even death
- disrupt schools and communities.

Why people join gangs

Gangs can make young people feel they belong and are part of something. They can support young people who might otherwise feel lonely or left out.

Some children grow up in a gang and stay with them or join other gangs as they get older.

Why join a gang?

Here are some reasons for joining a gang:

- To feel accepted.
- To feel safe and protected.
- To get respect.
- To have fun together.
- Because of boredom.
- To feel like you belong.

Replacement families

For some children, a gang can be like a replacement family. The young person may have no father at home and the mother may be busy at work, as well as bringing up several children. Many children grow up with little money in areas where there is not much to do. Some children may suffer neglect at home, or even violence or abuse.

Respect

In some neighbourhoods, if a father or older brother belongs to a gang, younger children will be expected to follow him into the same gang. Many children feel that belonging to a gang is a way of getting 'respect' from their own age group. Having all family members in a gang is another way of getting respect.

IN FOCUS

Role models

Children need someone to look up to as they grow up. These role models can be parents, older brothers or sisters, or celebrities like sports, pop or TV stars. On the streets, boys growing up without fathers often look to older boys in a gang as role models. Some gangs call these boys 'olders'.

Dilemma:

Ben's dad belongs to a gang on their estate, and his older brother is a gang member now. Ben's brother has told him he must join them but Ben has seen his brother come home with bruises. What should Ben do?

ROLE PLAY: GANG SAFETY

These people have very different views on gangs. Take one of the arguments and follow it through.

1 "Belonging to a gang keeps you safe. You are never on your own. There is always someone looking out for you."

Gang member, Shareen

2 "Joining a gang puts you at risk. You can be picked on by other gangs and get into fights with them."

Gang member, Nathan

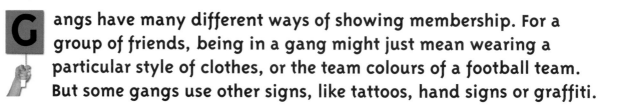

Looking alike

Gangs have many different ways of showing membership. For a group of friends, being in a gang might just mean wearing a particular style of clothes, or the team colours of a football team. But some gangs use other signs, like tattoos, hand signs or graffiti.

Uniform

Gang members often like wearing the same sort of clothes so that they look alike. In some gangs, everyone has one shoelace untied, wears the same design of T-shirt, or has one sleeve rolled back. Gang members may also have tattoos and personal belongings showing gang symbols, or their own nickname in the gang, such as 'Pirate' or 'Blanco'.

Street gangs

Street gangs, sometimes called 'crews', usually have leaders and followers, with older and younger members. New members may have to show how tough they are before they are allowed to join. It can be like passing a test. The leaders may be older or stronger than the others, but sometimes they are just bullies who like to control others.

In some gangs, all the members wear 'street fashion' like hoodies, baggy trousers and trainers.

Graffiti

Some gangs use graffiti to mark out their area or to make threats against rival gangs. The words or pictures often contain gang nicknames and can mark the scene of a crime. The graffiti may also advertise drug dealing.

Graffiti is sometimes used to commemorate dead gang members.

ARGUMENTS FOR AND AGAINST GRAFFITI

FOR!

- It can brighten up ugly areas.
- It is street art.
- It lets young people express themselves.
- Some graffiti artists become famous.
- It can be used to celebrate and commemorate.

AGAINST!

- It costs the tax payer money to clean up.
- It can be rude and offensive.
- It can carry gang threats.
- It can make places look scruffy.
- It is a form of vandalism.

IN FOCUS

Hand signs

Gangs use hand signs to greet each other, or flash warnings or threats to other gangs. They call this 'stacking' or 'a walk'. They use fingers on one or both hands to make signs that have meaning, like 'power' or 'number one'. Some use special handshakes among themselves.

YOUR CALL Some people think hooded tops (hoodies) should be banned from shopping centres because they hide faces and encourage crime. Would you wear a hoodie in a shopping mall when you know people are worried by them?

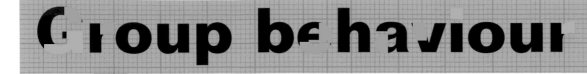

Group behaviour

P eople often behave differently when they are in a group. Being in a crowd makes them feel stronger and more confident but it can also make them feel more powerful. Some gangs use their power to make others feel uncomfortable or afraid.

School gangs

Some school gangs are harmless groups of friends. Other school gangs can make life difficult for pupils and teachers. Gangs can use peer pressure to make others join them and do things they don't feel comfortable with. They can bully younger pupils or anyone who is 'different' because of the way they look, sound or dress. Gangs can encourage each other to miss lessons or disrupt them, and cause trouble in the playground. Most schools have ways of dealing with problem gangs.

Public places

Gangs often hang around together on streets or in shopping centres. Some shops and public places are trying to discourage gangs of youths from gathering. They play classical music or use a device called the Mosquito. This makes a nasty high-pitched noise that only young people can hear.

Some schools have regular bag searches to stop weapons coming in.

If you knew a gang was bullying someone in school, would you do anything about it?

ROLE-PLAY: THE MOSQUITO

Some public places use the Mosquito to discourage young people from hanging out but others think this is unfair. Follow one of the arguments through.

1 "Shoppers can be put off by gangs of youths hanging about. They just don't feel safe. Anything that discourages gangs has to be a good thing."

Shopkeeper, Tamal

2 "It's not fair because the Mosquito only affects young people. How would people feel if they did something like this to old people? It doesn't just target troublemakers, it targets all young people."

Teenager, Jen

? **Dilemma:**
Sasha was pleased when she was asked to join a gang at her new school. But now they are encouraging her to skip lessons. Sasha doesn't want to get into trouble, but she is afraid of what the gang will do if she says no. What should she do?

A shopkeeper checks the Mosquito which he hopes will stop gangs gathering outside his shop.

Peaceful gangs

 Many people enjoy belonging to a gang. This doesn't mean that they have to get in trouble. Gangs can provide support and friendship for people who might otherwise feel lonely or unhappy.

Avoiding trouble

There are few places for young people to meet up except out in the street, or in public parks. However, older people, or even other children or teenagers, can find large groups of young people frightening. There are ways to avoid this:

- Only meet where it is allowed. Avoid badly-lit areas.
- Leave your meeting place clean — pick up your litter and mess.
- Don't shout out at people who are passing by, even if you are only having fun with your friends.
- Keep your face visible. Don't hide inside your clothes as people passing by find it alarming.
- Walk away from trouble.

Gangs do good

It can be boring in a gang if there is nothing to do and you do not have much money to spend. Some gangs decide to use their time to change their lives. They might plan a project to raise money for charity, or work with the local youth centre to set up activities that are of interest.

'The Pink Ladies' are a school girl gang who have fun together in the musical *Grease*.

These young people are helping to build a viewing area for a wildlife pond.

Green gangs

A group of young people can change a local area, even if they are still at school. Gangs can get involved with cleaning up the local area or working on a community garden. Some wildlife trusts have regular events for teenagers where they can learn skills and help the environment. 'Green gyms' have become another popular way of getting exercise and keeping fit at the same time as caring for the countryside through conservation projects, or working on allotments.

RESEARCH IT YOURSELF

There are lots of ways of ganging up with others that can be fun and creative. Find out about local groups in your area including sports teams, choirs, drama groups or conservation groups.

 Some people think more money should be spent on amenities for young people. What would you like to see in your area?

Violent gangs

Some gangs want people to fear them because they think it gives them respect and power. They may feel that it is only by making others afraid that they can get control over their own lives.

Some gang members walk around with fierce dogs, which can make other people feel threatened.

Fear

Gang members can shout at people, swear at them or insult them to upset them or make them feel afraid. This is often directed against rival gang members, but it can also be against anyone who annoys them, gets in their way or tries to stand up to them.

Physical violence

Gangs can be violent; mugging people or beating them up. They think this shows strength and power and will earn them respect. They may get hold of objects, including golf clubs, hammers or fence panels, to use as weapons to threaten and hurt others. Some members carry knives or even get hold of guns illegally (see pages 20–23).

RESEARCH IT YOURSELF

It is illegal to own certain breeds of dogs because they can be dangerous. Find out which breeds are banned and what the penalties for owning them are. You could look at: www.defra.gov.uk.

Some gangs go looking for trouble and are ready to pick a fight, especially when they out-number the victim.

Fights

Fights can start anywhere — on the street, on a bus or in a shop. Often they are sparked off by something very small, such as a look or a remark. Drinking alcohol and taking other drugs can make young people feel more violent towards others and often fights can break out on the streets outside bars or nightclubs.

IN FOCUS

Rap music

Rap music is a type of pop music where rhyming words are chanted over music with a strong beat. It has been around since the 1980s and is popular with many age groups. Some raps tell violent stories of gang attacks or violence towards women. This is why rap has been blamed for encouraging violent gang behaviour.

Dilemma:

A gang at Sophie's school wanted her to join them. Sophie said no because she knows the gang is violent and often get into trouble with the headteacher and even the police. Since then, the gang has been picking on her, stealing her textbooks, calling her names and making her life miserable. What advice would you give her?

Girl gangs

Girls join gangs for different reasons. Some become part of mixed-sex gangs; others join all-girl gangs. Often they are groups of friends who share the same taste in fashion, music or other interests.

Staying safe

Being in a gang can help give girls confidence when they are growing up. New situations, such as changing school, making new friends or joining a sports club, can be difficult when you are alone. Joining a gang can help girls have the confidence to get more out of their lives. Girls can also keep each other safe, especially at night, by sticking together or by talking through problems. It is always important to remember that others can feel threatened by a big group, however, whether they are boys or girls.

Many girls feel happier going out to clubs or parties, or just hanging out, in a gang.

Drinking too much alcohol can make emotions stronger and lead to fighting. Just two cans of a medium-strength lager contain more units of alcohol than are recommended for women to drink in a day.

Bullying gangs

Some girl gangs use the power they feel together to bully others. Girls in these gangs can get into fights with rival groups. Some say they get a feeling of excitement, or a 'buzz', from fighting, even when they get hurt. To join this kind of gang, a girl may have to prove herself by being mean to someone or taking part in a fight.

Binge drinking

Some teenage girls can see risky behaviour, such as binge drinking, as a way of appearing grown up and cool. They may see television reports about pop stars using drugs or getting drunk, and follow them as their role models. Groups of girls getting drunk and rowdy is a growing problem. Alongside the health problems it causes, drinking too much alcohol can make people feel angry or jealous, and can lead to fights and other bad behaviour.

ROLE-PLAY: HOW SHOULD GIRLS BEHAVE?

Here are two opinions on girls behaving like lads. Take one of the arguments and follow it through.

1 "Girls just want to go out together and have a good time. What's wrong with that? I don't think it's fair when people criticise girls for behaving more like lads. Why should lads get away with it?"

Teenager, Hannah

2 "Seeing girls swearing and getting into street fights makes me feel sick. Just because boys do it, why do girls feel they have to be like them?"

Community police officer, Mel

Turf wars

In big cities and some towns, gangs can base themselves around certain areas, estates or postcodes — their 'turfs'. Violent gangs or 'crews' defend their territory with knives or guns and fight 'turf wars' with rivals.

Fighting

Fights can break out across boundaries between rival gangs. The boundary can be a patch of land between two housing estates, or even the other side of a street. Gangs call straying into another gang's territory 'slipping'.

No-go areas

In some areas, young people are forced to stay close to home or risk getting attacked. They might have to take a long way round, catch a bus or get someone to drop them off to avoid trouble. Just crossing to the other side of a street can result in a mugging. Sometimes the attacker uses a mobile phone to round up others in the gang. Postcode gangs can 'rule' an area, affecting not just rivals, but everyone in a community.

Innocent victims

In recent years, a number of young people have been killed when they accidentally got into a dispute with a gang. These deaths are usually the result of gangs carrying knives or guns. Sometimes the victim is just in the wrong place at the wrong time.

IN FOCUS

Postcode gangs

Postcode gangs take their name from a postcode, such as E9, and then try to control the area within that postcode. They may use mobile phones with Internet access or GPS to check gang boundaries. They use graffiti to mark their own territory or to boast that they have strayed onto another gang's patch.

Mobile phones are used by gang members to swap information and map out their patch.

Clashes between gang members can result in serious injuries and even death.

ROLE PLAY: TURF WARS

Here are two different opinions on turf wars. Take one of the arguments and follow it through.

1 "It is about respecting territory. It's your neighbourhood. Often it's all you've got that belongs to you."

Gang member, Ryan

2 "Everyone should be free to go where they want. It's stupid to attack someone just because they come from the other side of the street."

Trainee police officer, Sean

Knife crimes

The number of knife crimes committed by young people on city streets is growing. More and more teenagers are carrying knives, even though it is against the law. However, despite the scary headlines, the risk of being stabbed is very low.

Staying safe?

Teenagers who carry knives often claim they need them to stay safe on city streets. They say carrying a knife means others are less likely to attack them. They think knives can be used to scare people away or to hurt someone without killing them. But stabbing often leads to accidental death and a growing number of teenagers are killed by knives every year. The evidence shows that carrying a knife makes someone more likely to become a victim.

Illegal knives

Although many countries have laws to prevent knives being sold to children, under-age teenagers still manage to buy them from shops or on the Internet. It is illegal to carry many types of knife, including flick knives, butterfly knives and knives disguised as something else. It is also against the law to carry any knife or sharp object, without a good reason, that could be used to threaten or hurt someone. Gang members often carry many different types of knife, from daggers and samurai swords to ordinary kitchen knives and meat cleavers.

The parents of a victim of knife crime in London lay flowers for their son.

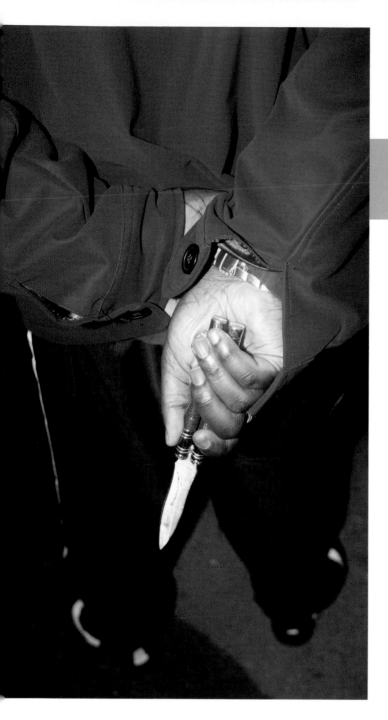

Butterfly knives like this are often hidden in clothing.

Knife amnesties

Sometimes the police hold a knife amnesty. They place safe bins in police stations, schools, youth clubs or churches. Thousands of knives may be handed in. There is often a fall in the number of knife crimes after an amnesty, but some police reports suggest they rise again within weeks.

At what age do you think children are old enough to be charged with a crime and punished for it?

Police powers

The police have stop and search powers to find anything that could be a weapon. Sometimes they use metal detectors. Young people caught carrying knives can be arrested and given a warning, or charged in court. There have been calls for tougher knife laws and penalties, including longer prison sentences.

Dilemma:

Jason has seen a knife in someone's school bag. He knows that it is against the law and against school rules. What should he do about it?

Gun crimes

There are tough laws on owning and trading in guns. But some gang members get hold of guns by buying them illegally on the street or over the Internet. They see guns as giving them power and status. They exchange pictures of themselves holding guns on websites or mobile phones.

Guns

Violent gangs see guns as 'clean' weapons because they can kill from a distance, unlike knives. They can use them to carry out armed robberies or mug people for money, phones or jewellery. Gangs also use guns to threaten rival gangs or carry out revenge killings. Often these gangs are dealing in drugs, which means big sums of money can be behind the killings.

Some handguns and ammunition are illegally imported from countries which have less strict gun laws.

Some violent gangs use guns to threaten or mug people.

Causes

There are many reasons why gun crime is increasing. Some people blame the fact that many young boys have no positive role model in their lives. Their heroes are the gun-carrying stars of violent films and console games. Other people blame troubled home lives, drugs, racism and peer pressure.

Some games have an adult rating because of violent content which can be upsetting for children.

ROLE-PLAY: VIOLENT GAMES

Here are two views on the influence of violent console games. Take one of the arguments and follow it through.

1 "It's no wonder that these kids think nothing of killing. They watch mindless games where people are blown to pieces and the whole aim is to shoot, injure and kill."

Youth leader, Jason

2 "It's silly to blame computer games. Kids know the difference between a game and reality. The kids watching games on their computers are not the ones out on the streets with real guns killing people."

Games designer, Ricky

IN FOCUS

Anti-gun music

Whilst some pop stars have been blamed for glamorising gun crime, others are leading a new wave of anti-gun music. These songs are trying to give young people a different message about guns and the damage they can cause. Often the pop star has been personally affected by gun crime, and has experienced the violent death of a friend or member of the family.

Social crimes

S ome gangs turn to crime to get money and to impress their friends. Crimes such as vandalism or arson (setting fire to buildings), tearing down fences or joy-riding cars are a way of showing off to each other and to rival gangs.

Cars are sometimes stolen for joy-riding, then wrecked or burnt out.

The Internet

Violent gangs often use their own web pages or social networking sites to brag about crimes they have committed. They also post photos or videos which show gang members committing crimes, such as vandalism and joy-riding. The web pages often display gang colours, clothes, graffiti and hand signs.

RESEARCH IT YOURSELF

The police offer protection to people who give evidence about crimes. Find out how this witness protection works. You could look at: www.bbc.co.uk/crimewatch/support/rav _specialmeasures.shtml

Young people see the 'red carpet' lifestyle and want it for themselves, but they look for fast and easy ways to get rich.

Grafting

Young people see football and pop stars, or even gangsters in their own community, living fantastic lives with big cars and lots of money. They want to be like them, so they look for quick ways to get big sums of money. They don't want to do low-paid jobs so they turn to crime. They might get involved in robberies, drug dealing or selling themselves for sex to get money. They call this 'grafting'. Gang members who are addicted to illegal drugs often use shop lifting and mugging as a way of getting money to buy drugs.

ROLE-PLAY: CAUSES OF CRIME

Here are two different views on why some gangs turn to crime. Take one of the arguments and follow it through.

1 "It's not surprising that kids turn to crime. The media is full of celebrities living millionaire lifestyles. Crime is the only way they see of getting what they want."

Journalist, Rhiannon

2 "Kids have a lot more today than they did years ago. They never used to have things like bikes and MP3 players and mobile phones. The difference is that many kids today don't feel loved or cared for."

Social worker, Danny

Safer streets

The police have powers to stop gangs causing trouble on the streets. Campaign groups and charities for victims or relatives affected by gang crime also work to stop gang violence and make the streets safer for young people and their communities.

Police powers

When gangs of youths gather in large groups, it can make other people feel scared. In areas where gangs have been causing trouble, police may have powers to break up a group and move them on. If gangs are not in their home neighbourhood, they can be stopped from coming back for 24 hours.

Curfews

Some city areas have curfews. This means that all young people who are not with an adult should be home between the hours of 9pm and 6am. The police have powers to take children who are breaking the curfew home. If there are problems with gun and knife crimes, police can use special squads and convoys of vans to patrol streets and discourage young people from getting into fights.

YOUR CALL What do the police do in your local area to make people feel safer? What else do you think they could do?

ROLE-PLAY: CURFEWS

Here are two opinions on curfews for young people. Take one of the arguments and follow it through.

1 "Curfews are a good idea because I am scared to go out because of all the gangs and people hanging around."

Teenager, Leah

2 "It's not fair on kids who don't do anything wrong. Often it's the older teens who are doing bad stuff, and it's not fair keeping everyone indoors because of them."

11-year-old, Ali

Talks and mentors

Police officers, ex-gang members and relatives of victims go into schools, youth clubs and neighbourhood groups to talk to young people about gang crime and the effects it can have on families. There are also schemes for young offenders in youth custody and prisons, where ex-gang members become mentors. They talk to young people about problems in their lives, and why they became involved in gang crime. They can also offer their own ideas on how to move on and change their lives. Mentoring can work well because the young person feels this is someone who understands them and has gone through similar experiences.

Many counselling and mentoring schemes are run by volunteers. They can be quite challenging for the young offender, for example asking them to think about the point of view of their victims.

Youth projects

Getting involved in sports, music or drama or learning new skills can give young people a sense of purpose and stop them feeling bored and lonely. There are many projects that offer young people new interests to keep them away from problem gangs. They are led by youth outreach services, youth and street workers, social workers and the police.

Activities

Projects in sports, the arts and music can help young people develop self-worth and give them new interests outside gangs. Some projects befriend young people who are at risk of getting into serious trouble and offer them the chance to learn new skills, such as video- and film-making, graffiti art or repairing motorbikes. Young people who are on community orders, or who have been to prison, can join projects where they write their story and make a video or film about it. Many YMCAs run sports clubs for young people.

Holiday play projects can offer the chance to meet new friends outside the gang culture.

Counselling

Many schemes offer counselling to young people to help them deal with problems in their lives. There are also workshops which help to sort out differences between gangs or gang members, or which help young people learn how to deal with their anger.

IN FOCUS

Sports projects

Sport can be used to break down barriers between gangs living on different estates. Projects mix up children from rival estates so they learn to play together and work as a team.

ROLE-PLAY: GANG CULTURE

Here are two opinions on gang culture. Take one of the arguments and follow it through.

1 "Kids in gangs are often just bored. No money is spent on youth centres or places for them to go. There is nothing else for them to do."

Street youth worker, Alicia

2 "The kids who do drugs and commit gun or knife crimes are not going to turn up to a youth club to play ping pong. Someone needs to look hard at what has gone wrong in their home lives. That's where the problem lies."

Ex-offender, Carl

Team sports, such as basketball and football, can help build social skills as well as fitness.

Glossary

Abuse Behaving towards someone in a way that makes them feel uncomfortable or unhappy.

Addicted When someone needs something so badly they feel they can't live without it.

Allotment An area of land that is rented from the council and can be used for growing flowers, fruits or vegetables.

Binge drinking Drinking alcohol quickly in order to get drunk — perhaps five or more drinks in a short space of time.

Bully Using unpleasant or forceful behaviour against someone and trying to control him or her.

Butterfly knives A type of folding pocket knife with two handles that open like wings to reveal the blade.

Caution An official warning.

Community order A sentence by the courts that involves practical work for the community or some other sentence, but does not involve going to prison.

Conservation The protection of the environment and the natural things in it.

Convoys Groups of vehicles.

Curfew A rule that prevents someone leaving his or her home between certain times of the day.

Graffiti Pictures or words sprayed, painted or scribbled on walls or buildings.

Illegal Against the law.

Knife amnesty A period of time when knives can be handed in without penalties.

Mentoring Giving advice and guidance.

Mosquito A buzzer device that makes a high-pitched sound, heard most clearly by young people. It can make them feel uncomfortable.

Neglect Lack of proper care.

Peer pressure Feeling pressurised to act in a certain way by people of the same age.

Peers People of the same age group.

Racism Behaving differently towards someone because of race.

Samurai sword A type of Japanese sword.

Territory An area or patch of land.

Vandalism Deliberate damage to property.

Further information

Websites

www.childline.org.uk/gangs
Questions and answers about gangs from this children's helpline.

www.rizer.co.uk
A website all about children, the law and crime.

www.stoptheguns.org
The website for Operation Trident, the campaign against gun use by the black community in London.

www.phoenix.gov/police/kidsC2.html
A website from the US Phoenix Police Department with sections on gang awareness and drugs awareness aimed at children and teens.

www.gripe4Rkids.org
A website aimed at fighting problem gangs with lots of information on gangs in the United States, including the history of street gangs.

www.cyh.com
The website of the Australian Children, Youth and Women's Health Service. The teens' health section has useful information on gangs.

Note to parents and teachers: Every effort has been made by the Publishers to ensure that these websites are suitable for children, that they are of the highest educational value, and that they contain no inappropriate or offensive material. However, because of the nature of the Internet, it is impossible to guarantee that the contents of these sites will not be altered. We strongly advise that Internet access is supervised by a responsible adult.

Index